Original title:
Tropical Serenade

Copyright © 2025 Creative Arts Management OÜ
All rights reserved.

Author: Matthew Whitaker
ISBN HARDBACK: 978-1-80586-354-0
ISBN PAPERBACK: 978-1-80586-826-2

The Gentle Lull of the Ocean's Breath

A crab in a tux, what a sight to see,
Dancing on sand in the rhythm of glee.
Seagulls are squawking their daily ballet,
As fish flip and flounder, making their play.

The waves bring a giggle, a splash and a roar,
While sunbathers snore on the warm, sandy shore.
A flip-flop mischief, oh what a tease,
Tangled and twisted in a gusty breeze.

The palms sway with laughter, their leaves in a whirl,
As coconuts tumble, they roll and they swirl.
A beach ball bounces, skimming the tide,
While a sandcastle's prince takes an accidental ride.

In this land of sun where the fun never ends,
Laughter and sunshine are always good friends.
So raise your drink high, let the antics begin,
In the buoyant embrace where the silliness spins.

Breeze-Kissed Petals

In the garden, flowers play,
Dancing like they're in a ballet.
Bees buzzing tunes, oh so sweet,
While ants tap dance with little feet.

Sunshine chuckles on the grass,
Grasshoppers jump, just like sass.
Little frogs croak in delight,
Crooning songs under the moonlight.

The Lure of Lush Horizons

Parrots squawk with vibrant flair,
Swinging from branches, up in the air.
Coconuts drop with a thud,
While crabs tiptoe, leaving a dud.

Flip-flops squeak on sandy shores,
As dolphins peek through ocean roars.
A turtle's slow race, what a sight!
Winners get a fruit-filled night!

Symphony of the Starry Night

Stars twinkle like they've had a drink,
While crickets jump and frogs just blink.
Fireflies jitterbug in the dark,
Painting scenes like a vibrant spark.

Laughter echoes from a nearby spread,
As marshmallows roast, stories are fed.
Owls hoot with a nod and a wink,
As nighttime's magic makes us think.

Lush Labyrinths of Light

In this maze of greens and gold,
A monkey swings, all brave and bold.
With a swing and a twist, he grins,
While squirrels plot their acorn wins.

Rainbow fish dart, a splashy beat,
Turtles float by, all cool and neat.
As sunsets paint the skies with cheer,
We'll dance on waves, 'til dawn is near.

Aromas of the Dusky Evening

In the air, sweet fruits collide,
Pineapples dance, and mangoes glide.
Coconuts wobble, they laugh and sway,
While crabs in tuxedos waddle away.

Laughter bubbles like soda pop,
As the sunset takes a funny drop.
Banana peels slip, oh what a sight,
The stars join the show, twinkling with delight.

Mysteries Cradled by the Ocean's Embrace

The waves tell secrets in silly sings,
Shells wear hats like funny kings.
Octopuses juggle, what a show,
While dolphins giggle, putting on a glow.

Seaweed whispers in a playful tune,
As fish do the cha-cha, under the moon.
Crabs in sunglasses strike a pose,
While turtles snicker as the current flows.

Colors of a Rain-kissed Isle

Raindrops paint colors, splashes of cheer,
The parrots joke, 'What's that noise? Oh dear!'
Bright hibiscus bloom, they laugh and yell,
As colors join in, casting a spell.

A rainbow appears with a wink and a grin,
Tropical colors play hide and seek within.
The sun peeks out, trying to maim,
The clouds just chuckle, saying, 'Not today!'

The Violin of the Wind's Caress

The breeze hums a tune, quite out of place,
It tickles the leaves, gives branches a race.
Bananas sway, singing 'What's that sound?'
While monkeys giggle, swinging around.

With every gust, there's laughter in the air,
The kites join in, dancing without a care.
Tropical breezes, they play and tease,
As waves clap along, 'We're here to please!'

Dappled Light through the Leaves

In the forest, leaves do dance,
Whispers float, a leafy prance.
Squirrels gossip, birds just tease,
Nature's jest among the trees.

Sunbeams flicker, shadows play,
A lizard sneezes, 'Please, no day!'
Monkeys laugh, a playful show,
While ants parade in neat little rows.

Echoing Steps on Sunlit Shores

Footprints trace a sandy tale,
Crabs retreat, their shells turn pale.
Children's giggles rise like waves,
Splashing chaos that misbehaves.

Kites soar high, a colorful fight,
Seagulls squawk with all their might.
Someone's hat takes flight, oh dear!
Chasing it brings laughter near.

Hummingbirds and Twilight's Caress

A hummingbird buzzes with flair,
Dipping and diving, light as air.
In twilight's glow, the fireflies twinkle,
While frogs sing hymns and crickets crinkle.

A pomegranate falls, what a mess!
Sticky fingers, nature's jest.
Evening chats by the garden wall,
Where laughter echoes, and shadows sprawl.

A Kaleidoscope of Island Dreams

Colors burst like laughter's sound,
Coconuts roll, tumbling 'round.
Surfboards clatter, a comic crash,
While waves retreat with a sassy splash.

Breezes tickle, hats fly high,
While mangoes dangle, just nearby.
In this world of playful schemes,
Sun-kissed moments weave our dreams.

Vows Under a Hibiscus Sky

Two clumsy lovers lost their way,
Tripped on petals, oh what a play!
Wedded bliss turned into a chase,
As a breeze danced, playing a face.

Coconut drinks tipped over in cheer,
Laughter echoed, made all things clear.
Under hibiscus, they took a bow,
Who knew love could turn into wow!

Dance of the Floating Lanterns

Lanterns floating like jellybeans,
Drunken crabs join with clumsy scenes.
Balloons tied to a monkey's tail,
Together they all set sail.

Fish in tuxedos swim with flair,
While old sea turtles begin to stare.
With giggles echoing through the night,
The ocean dances, what a sight!

Caravans of the Coastline

Beach umbrellas crowded the sand,
While seagulls plotted their next grand stand.
Sunscreen squirt battles made quite a mess,
As picnics sprawled in joyful excess.

Frisbees flying, dodging a sunburn,
In this circus, the tides take a turn.
Caravans roll, a parade so wild,
With ice cream cones, a beach day styled!

Nightfall on the Sugar Sands

Stars twinkled like sugar, oh so bright,
While crabs hosted a dance under moonlight.
Sandcastles toppled, joined in the fun,
As laughter sparked with each setting sun.

Barefoot in sand, the world feels right,
Swimmers emerge from the ocean's bite.
With giggles and splashes, round the bend,
Nightfall whispers, let the fun never end!

Moonlit Reflections on Water

The moon winks at the fish below,
They giggle in the current's flow.
Stars toss confetti on the tide,
While crabs dance with a goofy stride.

A frog croaks jokes in the night air,
His friends all laugh without a care.
Splashing water, making a scene,
As if they're actors on a screen.

The night is young, the fun won't cease,
Even the seaweed sways with ease.
A dolphin snickers at the tease,
While jellyfish join in with a breeze.

Lullaby of the Hibiscus

A bloom sings softly to the bees,
'Take a break, enjoy the breeze!'
Their honeyed giggles fill the air,
As petals dance without a care.

The sun sets low, a vibrant show,
While lizards practice their cabriolet flow.
A butterfly takes a spin, oh dear!
And lands on a snail, who shrieks with cheer.

The garden's alive with tricks galore,
Even a gecko wants an encore!
With laughter that flows like sweet perfume,
Each flower sways within the bloom.

The Flutter of Exotic Wings

Bright wings flap in a comical race,
As they chase each other in a wild embrace.
One stumbles, flops, and laughs out loud,
While flowers nod in a colorful crowd.

A parrot squawks some silly rhymes,
While ants march on, keeping the times.
The air is thick with a joyful tease,
As it tickles leaves, rustling with ease.

The dance is on, what a sight to see,
In nature's realm, pure jubilee.
With each flap and flutter, oh, what a game,
With laughter igniting all in their name.

Secrets of the Sunlit Canopy

Up in the branches, secrets swirl,
Squirrels gossip, making heads twirl.
A wise old owl gives a knowing smirk,
While monkeys swing with some frantic quirk.

The sunlight giggles through the leaves,
As shadows play tricks and cause mischief thieves.
Parrots squawk about what they see,
While vines weave tales, perhaps a spree.

The forest hums a merry tune,
As beetles dance beneath the moon.
Each creature shares a laugh or two,
In this lively tale, all is anew.

Ballad of the Lantern-lit Path

Beneath the lamps, the crabs commence,
They dance a jig with odd suspense.
Their claws in rhythm, taps and clacks,
As shadows prance along the cracks.

A lizard struts with fierce delight,
In high-top shoes, its feet take flight.
It shakes its tail; it winks an eye,
What's next? A cartwheel? Oh my, oh my!

In the Warm Embrace of Dew

The morning sun, it spills its gold,
A chubby bee is feeling bold.
It makes a splash in coffee cup,
Sipping slow, then drinks it up!

The flowers giggle, twist, and sway,
A butterfly joins in the play.
They plot a prank on passing snail,
And watch him stream with utmost wail.

Bay of Echoing Whispers

In the bay, the fish hold court,
They chat of dreams and tales retort.
A parrot laughs, it drops a line,
'Twas only a joke, it's fine, it's fine!

The waves keep rolling, making bets,
And crabs in caps set group regrets.
They claim the title of the champs,
While seagulls scatter, sound the lamps!

Ascending Towards the Cherry-Red Horizon

Up the hill, the monkeys race,
With tiny hats, they set the pace.
A swing from branch to branch, they fly,
They toss their fruits up to the sky.

The sun descends, all painted pink,
A walrus sips from pearl-filled drink.
With laughter ringing in the air,
They cheer the day with joyful flare.

Swaying Dreams on a Breezy Night

Bamboo sways, the moon does tickle,
Seashells whisper, crabs in a pickle.
Stars giggle down from heights above,
As coconuts dance with all their love.

A parrot jokes in a colorful way,
While sandcastles shout, 'We want to play!'
Fish in the depths throw a splashy tease,
Even the waves are bouncing with ease.

Laughter ripples across the bright shore,
Waves in a race, they yearn for more.
Seagulls swoop down with a comic dive,
In this lively realm, all feel alive!

Colors of the Coral Reef's Lullaby

Under the sea, where colors collide,
A clownfish grins, takes you for a ride.
Bright coral blooms with a cheeky twist,
As sea turtles join in a dance off the list.

Jellyfish jiggle with glee and delight,
While starfish wink under beams of soft light.
Conch shells crack jokes, so silly and loud,
Echoes of laughter weave through the crowd.

Puffer fish puff, then giggle with glee,
Tickling their friends in the deep briny sea.
Anemones sway to a jovial beat,
Making sure all feel the joy in their seat.

Gathering at the Shoreline's Edge

On the sandy strip, friends gather round,
Building great towers, with laughter abound.
Seashells parade in a humorous flight,
While crabs like comedians dance with delight.

Frisbees take flight, soaring so bright,
Chasing the sunset with all of their might.
Picnics explode with fun and a joke,
As mischief bubbles in every sweet poke.

Kites in the air tease the excited crowd,
Wind whispers secrets, whispers so loud.
Waves crash jovially, splashing with cheer,
While sun-kissed friends spread warmth far and near.

Nightfall's Gentle Embrace

As night draws near, the stars start to play,
Fishes in finery come out for the sway.
Moonbeams chuckle, guiding a dance,
While sea sprites twirl, lost in their prance.

A long boat drifts, with lanterns aglow,
Dancing silhouettes put on quite the show.
Crickets join in, with their chirpy rhymes,
Creating a concert for all funky times.

The sound of the surf sings a lullaby,
While fireflies flicker, as minutes go by.
As laughter floats high with the crash of each wave,
In this cheeky realm, all spirits are brave!

Whispers of the Island Breeze

A parrot squawks a tune, so bright,
While coconut drinks bring pure delight.
With island hats and flip-flops too,
We dance around, just me and you.

The sandcastles sway, they start to lean,
A crab walks by, he's quite the scene.
The sun rolls in, it's time to play,
With giggles echoing through the day.

The palms all shimmy in the breeze,
Their leaves are flapping, oh what a tease.
We chase the waves and slip and slide,
Laughing together where fun can't hide.

A pineapple hat, so very bold,
The whole scene laughs, it's pure gold.
We sing along to a playful beat,
In this land where joy can't be beat.

Lullabies from the Palm Fronds

The night falls soft with a gentle hum,
A monkey swings, oh what a clumsy bum.
The stars above twinkle and wink,
As island dreams invite us to think.

With fireflies blinking, like little stars,
A pig in shades strums on his guitars.
The breeze whispers secrets of the night,
While crickets chirp a rhythm, just right.

A hammock sways with a sleepy sigh,
While lizards dance, oh me, oh my!
The palms sway gently, a lullaby,
As we laugh and dream under the sky.

From coconut cups, we sip and cheer,
With silly grins, we have no fear.
Laughter flows like a gentle tide,
In this paradise, joy's our guide.

Echoes of a Sunlit Shore

Shells line the beach, a treasure trove,
While seagulls caw, they just won't loathe.
A dolphin leaps with a joyful spin,
While we all shout, "Hey! Let's dive in!"

The waves roll in with a frothy cheer,
As beach balls bounce, oh what a sphere!
A sunburned nose, oh what a sight,
While sunscreen fights a losing fight.

We build a tower of sand and hope,
A crab decides to take first scope.
It tumbles down, a sandy surprise,
With giggles erupting, laughter that flies.

With sunset hues like a painter's brush,
The island dances, oh, what a rush.
We stroll along with footprints galore,
As echoes of laughter fill the shore.

Rhythms of the Ocean's Embrace

The tide rolls in with a playful splash,
A beach ball flies, it's a perfect crash.
We line up for sandcastle design,
With snacks galore, a feast divine.

A crab scuttles, wearing a hat,
While seagulls squabble, what's up with that?
The sun is bright, the drinks are cold,
With stories shared, oh, the laughter bold.

The waves shout out their bubbly tune,
As we all dance beneath the moon.
With every splash, our worries float,
Just free-spirited, we cheer and gloat.

So let's embrace this ocean's waltz,
With upside-down smiles, we share our faults.
In this playful paradise, we weave,
A tapestry of joy, where we believe.

Echoing Laughter of Ocean Tides

Waves crash with a giggle, oh my,
Crabs dance with a bubbly high.
Seagulls wearing shades and bling,
As they strut and chirp and sing.

Flip-flops flying, right on track,
Surfboards ready, no turning back.
The beach ball bounces round and round,
Everywhere, laughter is found.

Sandcastles rise like silly dreams,
Moat filled with fizzy soda streams.
Sunburned noses and cheeky grins,
Where the fun never truly ends.

Shells whisper jokes to the breeze,
As sunbathers lounge with such ease.
With each tide, a story to tell,
Of joyous moments, all is well.

Starlit Reflections in Still Waters

Stars winking over the night so clear,
Fish in the pond laugh without fear.
Floating on lily pads, what a sight,
Toads croak along, it feels just right.

Fireflies dance like bright little sprites,
Casting odd shadows in the moonlight.
Splash! A frog jumps in with a plop,
The water ripples, but the giggles won't stop.

Glow-worms scribble stories sweet,
With tiny whispers, they can't be beat.
A tranquil scene, but oh so funny,
As crickets chirp their songs, not honey.

Reflecting laughter on waters deep,
Jokes riding waves, while others sleep.
In starlit silence, the fun unfurls,
As nighttime twirls and softly swirls.

An Ode to the Wild Frangipani

Oh frangipani, fragrant and bright,
You giggle in colors, a pure delight.
With petals that dance in the playful breeze,
Making bees laugh as they tease.

Butterflies flit, doing their dance,
Amidst the chaos, they take a chance.
Your beauty is silly, that much is clear,
A flower that brings all the joy near.

In the garden, a curious cat,
Sniffing your blooms while doing a spat.
With every whisker, and every meow,
You giggle right back, "Oh, look at me now!"

Beneath the sun, you sway with glee,
As passerby stop and smile with a knee.
A wild bouquet of merry surprise,
Laughing petals under sunny skies.

The Pulse of the Island's Heart

The island beats with a cheeky flair,
Palm trees sway like they just don't care.
The rhythm of waves, a playful tune,
Even the sand holds a funny rune.

Turtles in shades try to hightail,
Dodging the gulls, oh what a fail!
With every stumble, they giggle and glare,
A dance-off begins, without a care.

Bananas in hammocks swing to the beat,
A carnival of fruit, isn't that neat?
Mangroves laugh as they twist and twine,
All join in, even the old sea vine.

Cocktails clink under the sunset's glow,
Toasting to life and the island's flow.
With each heartbeat, the fun starts anew,
Echoing laughter, a vibrant crew.

Warmth of the Evening's Glow

In the hammock sways a cat,
With a hat that's way too flat.
He thinks he's quite the star,
While sipping on a jar.

The sun dips low, the sky's a peach,
While iguanas try to reach.
The guacamole's got a twist,
A dancing chip that can't be missed.

A parrot cracks a joke so bright,
Beaks all laughing, what a sight!
The crickets play their tiny tune,
While stars peek out, oh so soon.

The moonlight brings a playful bite,
As shadows make the night feel right.
With giggles echoing through the breeze,
Who knew fun could be so easy?

Secrets Told by the Fireflies

Twinkling lights in the dark parade,
Tiny bugs with tricks displayed.
They whisper secrets to the night,
While dodging laughter in mid-flight.

A toad joins in, a croaky bard,
With tales of frogs and other starred.
He hops along, oh what a tease,
With jokes about his warty knees.

Fireflies giggle, zipping this way,
While turtles cheer, it's such a play.
The leaves above sway with delight,
As critters sing their songs so bright.

In this glowing show, all join the rhyme,
Nature's comedy—a timeless climb.
With winks and wobbles, the night delights,
In a dance of glimmering, silly sights.

Dreaming Beneath Canopy Shadows

In twilight's grasp, the leaves recline,
Spiders spinning webs so fine.
A chubby squirrel, with acorn pride,
Hiding goodies where they abide.

Beneath the ferns, a party grows,
With singing frogs and snoring crows.
A dance-off starts, oh what a sight,
As ants parade in the moonlight.

The bamboo sways, a tickling tune,
A monkey jumps to join the croon.
His tail a swing, he's quite the show,
Laughing hard at the ground below.

Dreams flutter through, on butterflies' wings,
With giggles woven in the things.
A lighthearted vibe wraps round the trees,
Where all of life dances with ease.

Laughter among the Raindrops

Pitter-patter on the leaves,
The rain's a jester that deceives.
With splashes round, the puddles gleam,
As children chase the water's dream.

A splash, a laugh, the fun does rise,
With rubber boots and bright white skies.
The ducks parade with waddle sway,
While umbrellas dance, come what may.

Rainbows pop, what a view!
Kites are flying, celebrating too.
A joyful sound, the thunder's beat,
As all the world finds rhythm sweet.

Among raindrops, laughter flows,
In the rain, who really knows?
Whether splashes or silly slips,
The joy of water always trips!

A Serenade from the Island's Soul

A parrot sings to a coconut tree,
The rhythm's wild, just wait and see!
Under the sun, with a pineapple hat,
A crab joins in, now how about that?

The fishermen dance, their nets in a twist,
While fish in the sea just can't resist!
They swim with flair, and a splashy cheer,
Is that a tuna, or just a seafarer's beer?

A lizard tells tales in the afternoon light,
Of wild parties that last through the night.
With flip-flops flying and laughter high,
Even the bananas shake their peels and sigh!

So raise your glass in this vibrant place,
Where nature and humor compliment grace.
From sunrise to sunset, let the joy unfold,
With every wave, another tale told!

Footprints in the Silvery Sand

A pair of flip-flops left on the shore,
Dancing with crabs who want to explore.
The tide giggles softly, a ticklish tease,
As clumsy tourists stumble with ease.

The shells all conspire, a gossiping crew,
Whispering secrets of sunlit hue.
Each step in the sand, a story to write,
As seagulls perform their aerial flight.

A sandcastle troupe, with moats full of brine,
Decorates the beach like a showbiz line.
With a waving flag, made of seaweed and grin,
They raise a toast to the joy they're in!

So laugh at the fuss and the footprints that roam,
In this seaside whimsy, we all find a home.
With sandy smiles and the ocean's embrace,
Life's goofy adventures we all gladly chase!

The Sheltering Arms of Nature

In the jungle, the trees wear crowns made of green,
Hiding a monkey with mischief unseen.
He swings from the branches, a jester so spry,
With a wink and a laugh, as he zips by!

The flowers all giggle, with petals so bright,
Their fragrance is a joke, a charming delight.
While frogs play the chorus, a ribbiting sound,
In nature's embrace, joy knows no bounds.

A turtle's slow dance, with moves quite absurd,
Keeps the others laughing without a word.
When the sun sets low, and shadows grow long,
In nature's arms, we all belong!

So here in the wild, with laughs all around,
Every creature's a friend, our hearts gently bound.
Let's dance with the breeze, under skies so wide,
With nature as our guide, let's enjoy the ride!

Tides of Emotion Beneath the Moon

The waves are giggling, a gentle sway,
Under the moon, they play and play.
With surfboards laughing as they glide,
Even the tide can't keep their stride!

The starfish winks, with a sparkly grin,
While dolphins race, eager to win.
Each ripple sparkles, with secrets at bay,
As the moon whispers, "Let's dance and sway!"

The sand dunes sway like a rhythmic song,
With shadows of night where we all belong.
As laughter echoes through the salty air,
In the luminescent glow, we have not a care.

So raise your voice to the sky so vast,
Wave to the moments, let go of the past.
With tides of emotion, we laugh till we swoon,
Under the spell of that luminous moon!

Symphony of the Swaying Reeds

In the breeze, the tall reeds dance,
Each one swaying, taking a chance.
They bump and giggle, oh what a sight,
Making music in the soft moonlight.

The crickets chirp a silly tune,
As fireflies join, a glowing afternoon.
They twirl and twist, all in a row,
The reeds are stompers, putting on a show!

A frog joins in, croaking away,
Adding humor to this grand ballet.
With every leap and every glide,
The reeds chuckle, bouncing with pride.

So let's all dance, don't be shy,
Wobble like reeds, reach for the sky.
In our garden, carefree and whacky,
Nature's rhythm makes us all happy!

A Canvas Painted in Sunset Hues

The sky is splashed with silly colors,
Pink and orange, it sweetly purrs.
Nature's paintbrush, oh what a tease,
Creating giggles in the swaying trees.

Birds in laughter, cheeky and loud,
Joking with clouds, feeling so proud.
Their feathers shine like a bright balloon,
Floating on whispers from the afternoon.

The sun winks down, wearing shades of gold,
"See my show!" it gleefully scold.
As shadows stretch and games begin,
Even the bananas wear a silly grin!

So let the evening do its dance,
Grab a friend, give joy a chance.
In hues of twilight, let's be absurd,
Laughing and playing, life is my word!

Beneath the Banyan's Embrace

Underneath that massive tree,
Where roots twist and turn, wild and free.
The squirrels play tag, oh what a fuss,
Chasing their tails, causing a bus!

Laughter bubbles, as raccoons peek,
With tiny paws, they play hide and seek.
In leafy greens, the pranks unfold,
As laughter's warmth banishes the cold.

A turtle snickers, all slow and sly,
"Catch me if you can," he talks to the sky.
With silly slips, they turn and bound,
In this haven, joy is found.

So gather 'round, take a seat,
Listen to the giggles, they can't be beat.
In the banyan's shade, all fun will chase,
With silly moments we warmly embrace.

Whispers of the Wind in Paradise

The wind carries chuckles, a gentle tease,
As it sweeps through the palm trees with ease.
It plays with hats, oh what a sight,
Launching them high, like birds in flight.

A parrot squawks, with flair and zeal,
"Who's stealing my snacks?" it lets out a squeal.
As laughter echoes, rolling like waves,
The island hums, it's wild and brave!

The ocean giggles, its tides in a loop,
Flipping shells up, joining the troop.
Frothy and fun, it wiggles around,
Creating a party, spontaneously found!

So join the whispers, don't be forlorn,
Kick back, relax, till the new day's born.
With joy in the breeze, let's feel the bliss,
In this paradise, you won't want to miss!

Serengeti of the Sea

In the ocean zoo, fish dance in spree,
They wiggle and jiggle, so wild and carefree.
A crab in a tux, top hat just right,
Sips on seaweed, what a comical sight!

The octopus juggles with shells all around,
While the dolphin dives deep, with a splash and a sound.
A seahorse takes selfies, strikes a new pose,
Flaunting its mane like a fancy grand rose!

A starfish tap-dances upon the soft sand,
Swaying with rhythm, it's all just so grand.
The clownfish crack jokes, always swimming in glee,
Their laughter's contagious, a party at sea!

As sunset unfolds, all creatures unite,
For a grand ocean ball, a dazzling sight.
Fish wear their best, it's a splashy charade,
In this vibrant realm, life's a silly parade!

Kaleidoscope of Colors in Paradise

Under bright skies, where laughter takes flight,
Parrots squawk jokes, in colors so bright.
A lizard in shades, with swagger to show,
Lays down witty lines as it struts to and fro.

The bananas in bunches giggle on trees,
As monkeys swing by, bringing giggles with ease.
The sunflowers sway, with faces so bold,
Trading puns with the garden, a sight to behold!

In a patch of green, grasshoppers leap,
Their jokes hop from leaf to leaf in a sweep.
While the flowers do blush, with every wisecrack,
No one can stay mad, it's an endless laugh track!

The breezy day ends with a rainbow of cheer,
As the critters all gather, the party's right here.
Under starlit whispers, they dance and they sing,
In this color-filled world, let the laughter take wing!

Melodies in the Mangroves

Beneath tangled roots, where silly songs bloat,
A frog with a hat leads the choir of the boat.
Crickets strum bars on their tiny old strings,
While the riverboat hums like it has golden wings.

With spoons made of shells, the raccoons take part,
Adding the beat, oh what a funny art!
A turtle in shades slowly grooves to the beat,
While the fish tap their fins and shake their small feet.

The egrets all sway, with a dance in the breeze,
Twirling and whirling, oh what a tease!
The reeds sway along, in rhythm they sway,
Singing silly sonnets at the close of the day.

As fireflies join in, lighting up the stage,
The laughter erupts, the joy feels like a cage.
In mangrove's embrace, they twirl till they rest,
For the night is alive, oh what a jest!

The Chorus of Coral Reefs

In coral archways, where the fish make their home,
A sea cucumber gleefully starts to roam.
With a grin and a wink, it gives the seaweed a nudge,
Like, 'Hey, don't be shy! Let's dance, let's judge!'

The clownfish presents, fishy hats made of shells,
Joking with tangs as the magic swells.
A puffer fish floats in, all puffed up with pride,
Says, 'You think you can catch me? Go on, just try!'

With turtles who flip like they've lost their last bet,
And dolphins who surf like they've just found the net.
Every color a giggle, every fin a delight,
In this coral concert, laughter takes flight!

As night shimmers soft, the corals all gleam,
With fish floating by as they bubble and dream.
Together they blend, in giggles galore,
A chorus of joy that forever will soar!

Breath of the Island Night

With coconuts dressed in tuxedos,
The parrots start their show,
They dance with sway and wobble,
While the moon steals the glow.

A crab in a top hat struts,
Claiming he's the king's best mate,
He tumbles and rolls with glee,
Never realizing his fate.

The stars laugh and twinkle bright,
As the waves tickle the shore,
A lizard on a surfboard,
Claims, "I can surf like before!"

So grab your drink with an umbrella,
Join the party on the sand,
For tonight we'll sing and dance,
In this wild, enchanted land.

Wandering Through Emerald Isles

Frogs croak a jazzy beat,
As fish flaunt their scales in style,
A coconut falls with a splat,
It makes us laugh for a while.

Seagulls belt their high-pitched tunes,
As iguanas wiggle their tails,
We dance like we're on kazoo,
In this ship of giggling gales.

A snake tries to hula dance,
But ends up in a twisty mess,
While my flip flops won't stay put,
Causing everyone to guess.

The sunset wraps us in bliss,
With antics sweet and absurd,
When you're free under these skies,
Life gets really quite stirred.

Dreamscape of the Indigo Waves

A fish with glasses reads the news,
While dolphins break for cheer,
They giggle and tickle the surf,
Oh, what a sight, oh dear!

A crab in a hammock snores loud,
As jellyfish float with flair,
They pull pranks on passing boats,
As sailors pull out their hair.

The sandcastles wear crowns of seaweed,
Cheering for the best DIY,
While waves play tag with our feet,
Under the vast, open sky.

And if you join the fun with us,
The laughter floats on the breeze,
For in this dreamland of silliness,
We do just as we please.

The Kiss of Salt and Sand

A crab steals my picnic lunch,
As seagulls eye my fries,
I chase him across the shore,
To steal back my little prize.

The breeze tickles my sunburned nose,
While sunscreen's lost its fight,
A flip-flop's now a floaty boat,
Drifting further out of sight.

Sunsets lure us into dance,
With shadows stretching long,
We twirl and spin like wind-up toys,
As the waves hum a goofy song.

Tomorrow we'll laugh at today,
With salt crusted on our brows,
For in this land of giggles bright,
Joy's the sweetest of vows.

Azure Skies and Golden Fields

Under the sun, the cornflakes wave,
Chickens in hats, oh what a rave.
Cows in sunglasses, strutting with glee,
Dancing in rows, as happy as can be.

The sky is blue, matching their mood,
Squirrels wear boots, acting so rude.
Birds on scooters zooming around,
Chasing the breeze, not making a sound.

A picnic table with ants on a quest,
Frogs in a band sing their very best.
With laughter bright, the fields are a stage,
Join in the play, it's all the rage.

So come take a look, don't be shy,
Dance with the daisies, give it a try.
With cows and cornflakes, life isn't bland,
In the golden fields, come take my hand.

The Rhythm of the Nightingale's Call

Under the moon, the nightingale hums,
With crickets and frogs, the chorus drums.
Dance with the shadows, sway left and right,
Chasing the stars, it's a whimsical night.

Cats in tuxedos gossip away,
While mice in top hats plan for a play.
Fireflies twinkle like diamonds above,
Casting a glow on this night full of love.

The nightingale bursts into a fit,
With a twirl and a spin, it's quite a hit.
Worms in tuxes breakdance on grass,
As the owls blink on, letting time pass.

In this sweet chaos, laughter does rise,
With each silly note, joy occupies.
So sing with the night, let your spirit roam,
In this symphony, we all feel at home.

Dunes of Serenity in Twilight's Embrace

The sand is soft, like powdered sugar,
Lizards in scarves, oh how they snicker.
Kites in the air, flying with mirth,
As the sun sets, it's a comedy birth.

Tumbleweed dances, a real goofball,
While camels in hats invite one and all.
The dunes roll gently, like a soft quilt,
Where giggles and sandcastles are beautifully built.

Seagulls in sunglasses squawk out of tune,
Chasing the waves beneath the bright moon.
Kids in flip-flops, a fashion delight,
Splashing around, creating pure fright.

With laughter resounding, the dusk draws near,
An endless buffet of joy and good cheer.
So grab your towel, come join the spree,
In dunes of delight, just you and me.

The Dance of the Puffing Clouds

Up in the sky, the clouds wear a crown,
Puffing out shapes, swirling all around.
A bunny hops by, then a giant shoe,
A giraffe with a scarf in a whimsical hue.

The wind starts to giggle, tickling the trees,
While clouds play tag with their fluffy degrees.
The sun peers down, cracking a grin,
As raindrops in hats prepare to begin.

The clouds twirl and twist in a soft ballet,
A light-hearted show, come join the play.
With each little pffft, they stealthily glide,
In their cornflower kingdom, let joy be your guide.

So lift up your spirits, look high above,
The clouds are a canvas, painted with love.
Join in their dance, let your worries float,
In this sky-high circus, wear laughter's coat.

Memories Carved in Silhouettes

In the sun, we danced like fools,
With coconut shells turned to stools.
Laughter echoed in the air,
As flip-flops flopped without a care.

Caught a crab that stole my snack,
He scurried quick; I chased him back.
With sandy toes and sunburned nose,
We posed like kings in silly clothes.

A hearse of leaves, our pirate ship,
We sailed along on a salty trip.
Lemonade dreams, so sweet and bright,
We tackled waves till the fall of night.

Each snapshot blends, a wild chase,
Memories dance in this sunny place.
Though time will flutter and fade away,
We still find humor in each bright day.

Canvas of Shadows at Dusk

Painted skies in hues of fun,
As shadows jog, the day is done.
A parrot squawks, it steals the scene,
While monkeys plot like they're in a magazine.

Ghosts of palm trees sway and bend,
Chasing crickets around the bend.
With giggles soft and rustling leaves,
We summon laughter, and it weaves.

Moonlit moments, giggling tight,
The fireflies join our silly flight.
We build a fort from driftwood grand,
In this enchanted, giggling land.

With shadows tall and smiles wide,
We count the stars, our joy our guide.
In this canvas where dreams unfurl,
We find our place in a twinkling whirl.

Songs of the Monsoon's Arrival

Raindrops tap a funny beat,
Puddles pop beneath our feet.
We race the clouds, shout "look, it's here!"
With umbrellas flipped, we show no fear.

Splashing colors in the street,
As thunder roars, we can't be beat.
Kites of socks adorn the sky,
And paper boats drift sailing by.

Each raindrop sings a playful tune,
While frogs perform a bubbly croon.
We twirl and spin till we all splash,
The world becomes a joyful bash.

With laughter in each silver spray,
We dance together, come what may.
And like the storms that drink the land,
We laugh and play, hand in hand.

The Last Light of the Day's Retreat

As sun dips low, we find our zest,
With sand in shoes, we start the quest.
We chase the twilight, giggling loud,
As if the stars shall join our crowd.

The waves are cheeky, splash and tease,
While crabs wear shells with utmost ease.
Flip a fish, make a silly face,
We're all kids in this magical space.

Yes, the sunset throws its final rays,
As night reveals its masquerade.
While shadows stretch in a funny show,
We skip and hop in the evening glow.

Each moment fades, yet laughter stays,
In memories bright through endless days.
With cheers and grins, we end the play,
In the charm of the last light's sway.

Flickering Firelight Songs

Beneath the palm, a fire flickers bright,
We dance with shadows through the warm, soft night.
A coconut falls with a thud on my head,
The laughter erupts, but still, I'm not dead!

The moths join in, cavorting with the light,
An awkward ballet, a truly funny sight.
In the breeze, marshmallows seem to roam,
While the crickets call, "Hey, take me home!"

A parrot squawks jokes that make no sense,
We laugh till we cry, our sides grow tense.
The flames keep a rhythm, a flicker, a tease,
As we nibble on snacks and sway with the breeze.

The night stretches on, with giggles galore,
As the stars waltz above, begging for more.
In this flickering glow, we forget all our woes,
For in merriment's arms, true joy always grows.

The Gentle Humming of Nature's Choir

Beneath the trees, where the wild things play,
A chorus of critters chimes in the day.
The frogs croak loudly, a quacking brigade,
While the bugs buzz harmony under the shade.

A lizard strums strings, though they're made of its tail,
While the ants march on in a comical trail.
The wind whistles soft, like a tickling tease,
Making the leaves laugh, dancing with ease.

The sun shines down, a spotlight on cheer,
As a squirrel drops nuts, its aim not so clear.
And somewhere nearby, a goat starts to bleat,
Adding to the symphony, oh, what a treat!

Nature conducts, with a grin on its face,
In this concert of giggles, we find our place.
Each sound intertwined in a joyous ballet,
A funny serenade, brightening the day.

Island Shores, Where Dreams Reside

On sandy shores, where the wavelets dance,
We build up our castles, not leaving to chance.
A crab scuttles by, with its sideways strut,
It seems quite sure of its royal ruts.

With sun hats on, we strut like the peacocks,
Trading beach tales while wearing our frocks.
The beach ball bounces to the rhythm of tides,
As the gulls swoop down with smirks for rides.

A treasure hunt planned turns into a mess,
Finding old flip-flops, each worn, I confess.
We stumble and trip, laughter filling the air,
As the sun sets low, turning gold to the dare.

With goofy grins, under stars shining bright,
We dance in the waves, a true silly sight.
In this playful place, where dreams come alive,
The humor flows freely, and spirits all thrive.

Roaming Beneath the Starry Canopy

Under the stars, we wander and weave,
With wishes and giggles as tricks up our sleeve.
A raccoon chuckles at our silly parade,
While we skip through the grass, every fear laid.

The moon plays peekaboo, a cheeky old chap,
As we hunt for constellations on the map.
"Is that a bear? No, just Auntie's big hat!"
Laughter erupts like we're all in a spat.

A nighttime game of charades with our mates,
Trying to act out the most curious traits.
The bats swoop low, participating too,
Undoubtedly pondering just what we'll do.

In whispers of night, under skies ripped with light,
We shrug off our worries, embracing the night.
In this woodland jest, where the laughter runs free,
We roam 'neath the stars, wild, happy, and free.

Harmonies from the Coral Shores

On the beach, the crab does a dance,
With a sideways shimmy that gives us a chance.
A fish in a bow tie swims by with flair,
Making waves like it just doesn't care.

Seagulls squawk tunes, in off-key delight,
While the shells join in, making music all night.
A conch shell whispers old sailor tales,
As a whale winks, with a blink that prevails.

Everyone gathers, it's quite the affair,
When a dolphin cartwheels, and we all just stare.
The tide comes in, but we stay on dry land,
With laughter echoing, it's a funny band.

So with maracas made from coconuts bright,
We play our own rhythms till the morning light.
A fiesta of laughter under the sun,
At the coral shores, oh, what silly fun!

Rhythm of the Tropical Rain

Pitter-patter drumming on the roof above,
A monkey swings by, showing some love.
Dancing in puddles with silly wet shoes,
A parrot yells jokes, what a colorful muse!

Frogs in tuxedos sing out in delight,
As lightning bugs flash, making night feel bright.
Raindrops are glistening like pearls on a string,
While the sloths slow dance, oh, what joy they bring!

The rain starts to swirl in a quirky ballet,
As the palm trees shimmy, catching rays of gray.
Each drop a giggle that tickles the ground,
Who knew that rain could be so profound?

So grab your umbrella, let's twist and twirl,
In a storm of laughter, let the fun unfurl.
The rhythm of the rain is a sight to see,
In this wacky wonder, let's all just be free!

Serenading the Evening Star

The sun waves goodbye, night takes the stage,
Crickets play melodies, feeling their age.
A firefly flickers with a wink and a smile,
While the owls hoot softly, lending their style.

The moon dons a hat made of silvery light,
As stars start to giggle, twinkling in flight.
A raccoon serenades with a guitar out of tune,
While the shadows dance under a bright, friendly moon.

Lizards in bowties take to the floor,
Doing the cha-cha, who could want more?
With each little step, they bring laughter and cheer,
As the night unfolds, every creature draws near.

So sing to the stars, let your voice flow free,
For the evening's a party, come join in with glee.
The joy of the night is a playful delight,
Serenading the skies till the morning feels right!

Essence of the Ocean's Heart

In the waves, a surfboard dog catches a ride,
While the octopus claps, feeling quite spry.
A turtle in shades, moving slow with class,
Waves hello, then does a smooth little sass.

The sandcastles rise like dreams in full bloom,
With a crab as the king, wearing a seashell crown's loom.

Seashells are gossiping, sharing the news,
Of dolphins in limos, rocking bright colors and hues.

A lobster plays poker; the stakes are quite high,
While a seahorse gives lessons, make waves and fly!
The beach is abuzz with fun all around,
Where laughter and silliness joyfully sound.

So feel the salt breeze, let go all your cares,
Join in with the fish and the sunshine affairs.
The essence of the ocean is humor and cheer,
In this aquatic kingdom, let's all persevere!

The Call of the Coral Coast

The waves sing out a silly tune,
As seagulls dance beneath the moon.
Crabs in tuxedos shuffle about,
Laughing as they scuttle without a doubt.

Flip-flops flopping on sandy shores,
With drinks so bright, who could ask for more?
A parrot squawks with a cheeky grin,
"Don't forget your sunscreen, let's begin!"

Sunburned tourists in a twist,
Missed their towels, oh what a tryst!
With ice cream melting on the floor,
They trip and tumble, laugh to the core.

The sun sets low, a fiery ball,
Even the fish are having a ball.
Underwater hide-and-seek, what a blast,
Just don't let the jellyfish be the cast!

Secrets in the Canopy Dance

In the treetops where monkeys wave,
Swinging and laughing, it's mischief they crave.
A sloth sips coffee, takes it slow,
While the parakeets put on a show.

Mango smoothies spill down the bark,
As toucans take aim with a silky arc.
The dancing leaves whisper tales of cheer,
But the ants march on, with bug-eyed fear.

Lianas twist like ribbons of fun,
While lizards sunbathe, basking in the sun.
A chameleon changes but not his grin,
Winks at the viewers, then jumps right in!

When night drapes velvet over the green,
Frogs croak the dormitory serenade scene.
Each creak and croon makes the forest prance,
In this wild and whimsical canopy dance!

A Driftwood Love Affair

On the beach, a tall, handsome log,
Caught my eye, but it looked like a hog.
With a sun-kissed ocean as our stage,
I felt a tickle, turned the page.

Sandy toes met splintered wood,
A love affair, misunderstood.
Seashells giggled as they passed by,
Whispering secrets under the sky.

A crab discreetly tried to spy,
On our romance as it waved goodbye.
With salty kisses and the tide's embrace,
We danced through the night, what a silly place!

When the tides pulled away, oh what a shame,
My driftwood love was no longer the same.
But in my heart, it made me smile,
A funny love that will last for a while!

Kaleidoscopic Sunsets

The sky bursts forth in colors so bright,
Like jellybeans fighting a berry fight.
As the sun dips low without a care,
Even the clouds say, "Hey, look, I'm rare!"

Frogs in the pond sing high-pitched tunes,
While fireflies flash like little balloons.
The horizon gets dressed in hues so grand,
Where pink elephants might just stand!

Children giggle, chasing the breeze,
Sandy hair tangled like twinkling trees.
Grinning, they collect shells in their bags,
While the sunset winks, playing pranks like jags.

Under the stars, laughter takes flight,
With dreams gliding gently into the night.
Kaleidoscopic colors will always stay,
In the hearts of those who love to play!

Ripples of Laughter on Gentle Waves

The parrot squawks a silly joke,
While surfers giggle, almost broke.
A seashell sings, but it can't swim,
As tides pull in on a whim.

The crabs all dance, with jiggly feet,
Using their claws, they keep the beat.
Fish in schools don party hats,
While dolphins prank the grumpy cats.

A beach ball flies like a big balloon,
As sandcastles melt to sudden gloom.
With each splash, the giggles grow,
As jellyfish join the funny show.

And when the sun sets, the jokes still flow,
With starfish telling tales that glow.
Every ripple hides a laugh or two,
On gentle waves where joy feels new.

The Hidden Garden's Serenade

In the garden, gnomes have fun,
Playing hide-and-seek with the sun.
Tulips gossip, waving their heads,
While daisies snicker in their beds.

Butterflies wear the brightest clothes,
Promenade on petals, striking poses.
Bees burst into laughter when they trip,
Buzzing songs from their honeyed lips.

A frog leaps with the biggest smile,
Croaking tales that will take a while.
The evening blooms with marmosets' chats,
Chasing shadows like playful cats.

As moonlight bathes the scene in grace,
The garden giggles, a happy place.
Each rustling leaf knows a chuckle or two,
In this hidden realm where dreams feel true.

Melancholy of the Setting Sun

The sun dips low, a golden ball,
The clouds gather like a drummy hall.
Yet crickets play their tiny lute,
Mice in tuxes dance, oh how they loot!

A wink from Venus, a laugh from Mars,
Fireflies twinkle like little stars.
While shadows stretch and whisper low,
Even the moon can't help but glow.

An octopus strums on seaweed strings,
Making music while seagull sings.
As twilight whispers sweetly to the night,
Much like a joke that feels just right.

Though the sun may sigh and softly fade,
In every shimmer, a joke is laid.
With stars to guide the playful dance,
Laughter lingers in every chance.

Laughter in the Breeze of Paradise

In paradise, the winds do laugh,
Tickling palms with a gentle path.
Coconuts chuckle with every bump,
As flip-flops squeak, a goofy thump.

The waves crash in a rhythmic cheer,
Where surfers wipe out without fear.
Hammocks sway as monkeys swing,
With ripe bananas, they start to sing.

A sunset paints the skies in hues,
While turtles wear their brightest shoes.
Breezes carry jokes from afar,
Tickling noses like a bright shooting star.

And as the stars peek down to see,
The laughter echoes, wild and free.
With every gust, hearts feel light,
In paradise, joy takes flight.

Ramblings of a Roaming Tide

The waves are chatting, oh so loud,
A seaweed party, gathering a crowd.
Starfish are dancing, with such delight,
While crabs join in, making it a fright.

The gulls are gossiping, quite the scene,
Stealing snacks, if you know what I mean.
A fishy ballet, beneath the sun,
Splashing around, oh, what silly fun!

Seashells are laughing, their stories untold,
In this salty gallery, treasures unfold.
The tide pulls back, then rolls on ahead,
Whispering secrets, like it's half-dead.

My rubber duck dances on the shore,
It squeaks and wiggles, who could ask for more?
With every wave and giggle I find,
I'm swept away by the ocean's kind.

The Allure of Azure Dreams

In a land where cucumbers wear little hats,
The fish gossip about the acrobatic bats.
Jellybeans float, and so do the pies,
As I dream of beachcombers, wearing their ties.

The sun chases shadows across the sand,
While pineapples chatter, isn't it grand?
Seagulls in tuxedos dance on the breeze,
How absurd and silly, oh, if you please!

In this vibrant cove, laughter sings high,
As waves flirt with buckets — oh my, oh my!
Kites take to the air, all colors ablaze,
Like rainbow-laden mischief, in whimsical ways.

I chase after shells, my eyes full of glee,
A crab in a top hat says, "Come dance with me!"
As the sun dips low, in a sweet display,
The laughter keeps soaring, it's a perfect day.

Lush Whisper of the Palms

Where coconuts giggle, and limbo is king,
The parrots are rapping, oh what joy they bring!
Cacti wear shades, reclining with flair,
While lizards debate, who's the fairest of hair.

In the gentle sway of the leafy parade,
Monkeys are swinging, their jokes well played.
Waves crash hilariously, a watery punch,
A beach ball deflates, in a comical crunch.

The sunflowers sway, putting on a show,
With seeds of humor, like popcorn they throw.
The gales keep the laughter, spinning around,
As palm fronds catch giggles from out of the ground.

A crab in a beret struts down the shore,
Sipping on coconut, craving some more.
With every bright breeze, mischief flows free,
In this silly oasis, oh so carefree!

Sounds of the Ocean Breeze

A chorus of conch shells, what a delight,
They trumpet their tales, day turns into night.
With every wave, a giggling frolic,
As clams plan a party, quite symbolic!

Lighthouses wobble when the wind starts to laugh,
Spinning in circles like a goofball giraffe.
Sandcastles tumble, with a playful crash,
As the surf shouts loudly, giving a splash.

In the warmth of the sun, pink flamingos prance,
In shiny pink suits, they join the dance.
While jellyfish waltz, gliding with ease,
In this whimsical world, set to the breeze.

The winds play their tune, a funny refrain,
While the ocean joins in, like a raucous train.
With smiles and chuckles, nature's grand show,
We laugh till we cry, in this bright ebb and flow.

Beneath the Frangipani Moon

The frangipani sways, oh so sleek,
Where bats wear suits and monkeys speak.
A lizard strums on a tiny guitar,
While crabs tap dance by the sea so far.

A starfish twirls with a wink and a grin,
Telling tales of the ocean's whim.
And here comes a parrot, trying to sing,
But can't find the notes, just does his own thing.

Drifting along like a jellyfish shy,
With glittering dreams as they pass by.
The moon casts shadows while laughter blooms,
In a garden of giggles, where joy consumes.

So let's toast to the quirks and their schemes,
In this land of wonders and silly dreams.
With friends all around in this fragrant space,
We'll tango with joy in this lovely place.

Songs of the Coconut Grove

In the shade of palms, coconuts cheer,
With melodies sweet and jokes to hear.
The owls wear glasses, look quite refined,
And sing to the crabs, who rhythmically twine.

A squirrel in stripes gives a quirky wink,
Selling fruit smoothies by the ol' pink sink.
The breeze joins in, with a giggle or two,
Whispering secrets to the daisies so blue.

Guitars made of shells strum tunes of the sun,
As the hermit crabs march, oh what fun!
Flamingos in socks prance with delight,
While the fireflies dance, embracing the night.

With laughter in waves, and joy in the fray,
Every critter joins, no one fades away.
Together they sing, beneath the sun's glow,
In the heart of the grove, where the silly winds blow.

Tango of the Tides

The waves come in with a bubbly jest,
Dancing with sand, oh what a quest!
Seagulls in tuxedos, oh what a sight,
Chasing fish tails till the end of the night.

A dolphin flips in a splash of delight,
As crabs do the conga, not quite polite.
With shells as their hats, they sway to the beat,
The rhythm of tides, oh what a treat!

In a swirl of foam, the starfish join in,
Their arms waving wildly, a flurry of spin.
Jellyfish jelly and shrimp in a line,
Move to a groove that feels oh-so-fine.

So let's all tango with the sea and the sun,
In a frolicking tide, where there's laughter and fun.
The ocean's an artist, painting our minds,
With strokes of humor, the best there ever finds.

Hummingbirds at Dusk

Little hummers buzz low, in a flurry of flair,
While the sun dips low, painting skies with care.
They sip nectar sweet from blossoms aglow,
Making faces at frogs putting on a show.

With tiny top hats, they flit to and fro,
Dancing on air while the breezes blow.
The moths join the party, in glittering twirls,
Spinning around in their silken swirls.

An old tortoise grins, moves slow with intent,
As fireflies light up like stars heaven-sent.
Together they giggle, oh what a scene,
In a garden where laughter reigns evergreen!

So raise up a toast with your fanciest cup,
To nature's own jesters who never give up.
For beneath twilight's soft, teasing glow,
Happiness flutters, wherever we go.

Foraging for Starfish Dreams

Beneath the seaweed, treasures lie,
Starfish giggle as they pass by.
They barter shells for tasty fries,
In this bizarre aquatic hi-fi.

Crabs in tuxedos, dancing brave,
Twist and twirl, not one to save.
They lose their shoes in playful waves,
As jellyfish sing from beneath their caves.

A clam plays cards, with quite a flair,
Betting pearls, without a care.
Fish flip flop, in swimwear rare,
While octopuses strut, a fashionable pair.

Dreams of snacks from golden sands,
As seagulls wait, with hungry hands.
In this ocean, laughter expands,
Foraging dreams where humor stands.

Oasis of the Sapphire Waves

In the oasis where the mermaids laugh,
Sea turtles sketch their favorite bath.
They sip on drinks from coconut halves,
Swapping tales of their underwater gaffes.

Dolphins, wearing shades so wide,
Surf the waves with perfect pride.
They slam dunk fish, with flips that glide,
Their humor's surely not to hide.

A parrotfish struts, a sight to behold,
In a tuxedo made of coral gold.
Even the starfish, looking bold,
Crack jokes 'til the sea is cold.

With every splash and every cheer,
Life's a carnival, let's be clear.
In sapphire waves, so brilliantly sheer,
Laughter floats, and joy is near.

Prism of the Sunset Glow

As the sun dips in a fiery blaze,
Octopi play in funky ways.
They twirl their arms in rainbow haze,
Then pose for selfies in this craze.

Crayons sing as colors dance,
The fish all join in a funny prance.
A sea cucumber joins with romance,
And whales throw parties for a chance.

The isotopes of color blend,
While clam-shells gossip, their voices send.
The coral reef, a vibrant friend,
Where every joke finds a happy end.

Glowworms gather, tales in tow,
Trading secrets in the golden glow.
A prism casts, what a splendid show,
In the sunset's arms, we laugh and flow.

Enchantment at the Water's Edge

At the water's edge, where crabs parade,
They dance on sandals, being quite frayed.
A pelican juggles, unafraid,
While seaweed whispers, jokes displayed.

Seashells gossip, sharing a grin,
As fish discuss where they've been.
The starfish play, a cool spin,
With mermaid laughter that's sure to win.

Drifting ducks don top hats grand,
Quacking riddles across the sand.
Shellfish clapping, isn't it bland?
They roll their eyes, it's all quite planned.

Under the sun, the smiles surge,
Wave after wave, a bubbling purge.
At the water's edge, where laughs emerge,
Enchantments grow like a joyful dirge.

www.ingramcontent.com/pod-product-compliance
Lightning Source LLC
Chambersburg PA
CBHW060123230426
43661CB00003B/313